William Richardson

The rabbit

How to select, breed and manage the rabbit for pleasure or profit

William Richardson

The rabbit
How to select, breed and manage the rabbit for pleasure or profit

ISBN/EAN: 9783337147143

Printed in Europe, USA, Canada, Australia, Japan

Cover: Foto ©Lupo / pixelio.de

More available books at **www.hansebooks.com**

THE RABBIT.

HOW TO SELECT, BREED AND MANAGE THE RABBIT
FOR PLEASURE OR PROFIT.

BY W. N. RICHARDSON.

CLARENCE C. DE PUY, PUBLISHER,
SYRACUSE, N. Y.

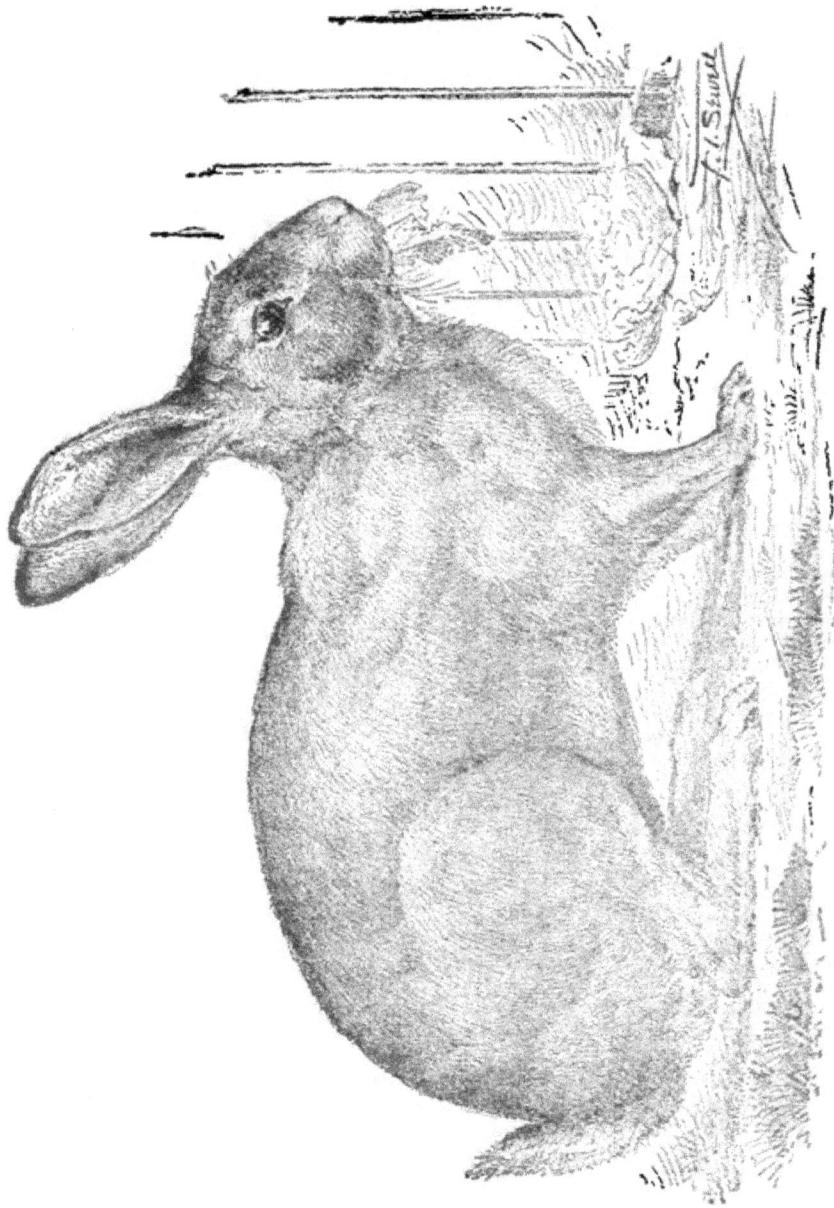

BELGIAN HARE BUCK "BUSINESS."

Owned by LEMUEL RICHARDS, Troy, N. Y., Receiving the Highest Award for Belgian Hares Exhibited at the WORLD'S FAIR, 1893.

THE RABBIT.

HOW TO SELECT, BREED AND MANAGE THE
RABBIT FOR PLEASURE OR
PROFIT.

——BY——

W. N. RICHARDSON

INTRODUCTION.

The demand for a hand book on the Rabbit, explaining in practical manner the mysteries of rabbit culture, treating especially on the care and management of the Belgian Hare, is the only excuse for perpetrating this volume on an indulgent public.

In the main the writer's actual experience is given; while for information requiring greater experience and familiarity with the Rabbit, such eminent authorities as Messrs. Watmough, Mason and Knight, of the land of fanciers, "England," are quoted.

If, by following the plans recommended, the privations and sufferings of an animal so noble, so worthy of good care and attention, are lessened, the knowledge of their increased comfort, will amply repay the trouble involved, and the mission undertaken will be crowned with success. Read this book carefully, follow the directions plainly given, and the result cannot be otherwise than successful.

THE AUTHOR.

RABBITS FOR PROFIT.

Most people in this country think that the rabbit is a use-less pet, and being unacquainted with their habits and possibilities, condemn them, as unworthy of the care and attention they so justly deserve.

The Rabbit question has its bright side. The formerly neglected rabbit is now furnishing both pleasure and profit when managed intelligently.

I find that nine of ten fanciers who give up, do so because they cannot keep their pets in proper health. There is a great deal in feeding, housing and mating.

The conclusion is, that, fanciers spend too much money in feeding their Rabbits giving them too much to eat and the consequence is that they either become diseased or there is a tremendous waste of food. As a rule they are kept in too small quarters, thereby generating disease for want of pure air, I am pleased to say that many men in the fancy have seen their mistakes and are now making the Rabbit a success financially.

There are Rabbits of all colors, sizes and conditions from which to select an ideal, which must possess many good qualities among which must be, a good appearance, large size, prolificacy, and hardiness, they must mature quickly, be exempt from disease and vermin, finally furnishing a delicacy for the table at a cost not exceeding their more popular rivals, Poultry.

THE RABBITRY.

One great essential to success is proper quarters for the stock, this building is called the rabbitry and is as easily constructed as an ordinary hennery and for number of occupants to be considered at a much less expense, the model Rabbitry will afford protection from moisture and storm, space for exercise and separation of the breeders, and all important will be ventilation, for when during the warm months sickness will sure to follow any lack of pure fresh air, plenty of windows, wide open, a large ventilator through the roof all tend to keep the place cool and free from unpleasant odors, secure a tight roof and a dry floor preferably of cement; bricks absorb too much moisture and render the rabbitry very damp in cold weather, a good board floor is quite acceptable if cement is not to be had, regarding the hutches there can be no mistake that the larger the better.

A breeding hutch should be not less than six feet long, two feet wide, and twenty inches high, partitioning off about twenty inches of one end for a nesting room, this apartment should be dark, with an entrance six inches wide at the front and extending from the bottom to the top of the hutch, thereby ventilating the apartment. A door eight or ten inches wide of the same height furnished with a suitable catch for the front, so as to admit a white wash brush easily, The front of the remaining forty inches should have a door of one inch mesh wire netting, fastened to a frame work of seven-eights by two inch wood, this door to be hinged at the end farthest away from the nesting apartment, the one inch mesh netting keeps in the young rabbits and keeps out *old rats*. If the partition between the living and nesting apartments is made so as to be easily taken out the hutch can be used by the growing brood until large enough to separate, always put the netting on the inside of the frame for often bunny will enjoy nibbling at the soft wood generally used. I sometimes put a small piece of wood in the hutch for them to wear down their teeth by gnawing upon it. A brood buck will be perfectly happy in a hutch five feet long and of course needs no nesting apartment. The hutches are best built two feet from the floor leaving that space for growing stock to run about in, for if you want those long racy specimens the standard demands they must have *exercise* and plenty of room to grow.

The food and water dishes must be securely fastened in place or the contents will be upset and wasted.

FEEDING.

What will a Rabbit eat? It would be easier to name what they would not eat. Hay, oats, corn, wheat, peas, barley, and in fact anything that a cow or sheep will, cabbage, beets, turnips, carrots, dandelion, milkweed, plaintain are a few delicaces, dry bread and milk, corn bread, boiled potatoes, raw onions, pea pods, green corn, and fresh cut clover for a desert. What else? every vegetable known to man except poison ivy or wild parsnip. The only thing required is a little judgment in the supply and the variety will be very acceptable.

Always have a supply of good clean hay and oats before them, give green stuff once or twice a day and only in quantities that will be eaten clean, in the summer large quantities of green food can be fed, our pets are delighted with the *fresh* cool succulent plants and the grain bill correspondingly decreases, a little care is needed to change from a dry grain diet to green food. The young juicy stuff freshly gathered has, on grain fed animals, a tendency to scour them,

but after they become accustomed to the diet they can be
supplied liberally.   In giving green food to youngsters care
should be especially exercised.

Always bear in mind that the fresher the better.
Trouble is caused by wet stuff being allowed to lie in
a heap, thereby steaming and sweating until unfit for
use, at the same time avoid wet green food if fresh and dry
food is procurable, remember that a heap of green stuff in
the hutch to be trodden upon and covered with filth, is to
my idea an unpardonable condition of affairs and is often the
cause of serious trouble.   Does nursing should have as much
as they can eat, green corn, carrots, fresh clover, etc., are
excellent milk producers and should be fed in conjunction
with sound whole oats, give cool fresh water twice a day
keeping it always before them.

WATER FOR RABBITS.

It is pleasing to know that there is no greater advocate than
myself in favor of giving rabbits water as a beverage.   I was
taught that water was to be used only as a remedy for diarrhœa, and, until recently employed it only as such; but see-
ing my pets drink their own urine, I concluded they were
thirsty and desired a drink of water.   Think of the numbers
of rabbits that are confined in generally too small quarters
that have to suffer through the hot summer months and the
feverish hours attendant upon giving birth to their young,
deprived of the costless yet essential requisite, "*a drink of
water.*"   To the adherents of the no water system, I would
advise the reading of this clipping concerning the rabbit pest
in Australia and how their extinction is conducted:

"In all but the remote sections, the rabbits are fairly under
control.   Millions of rabbits have been killed by fencing in

the water holes and dams during the dry season, whereby they die of thirst, and they lie in piles against the obstructions they so frantically and vainly strived to climb."—[*Mr. S. Dickinson, in Station Life in Australia*.

This, I think, should convince the most skeptical that water is beneficial, if not indispensable to a rabbit, particularly when in captivity and deprived of their natural juicy food. I will state that since adopting the water plan I have not had a sick rabbit in my rabbitry.

MATING.

Judicious mating is an essential to success in rearing any stock. Injudicious crossings are often resorted to, which result in no benefit.

The most common crosses met with are the Lop, the Flemish and the Patagonian; each cross showing distinctively its ancestors. The Lop is distinguished by its soft, pendulous ears; the Flemish by its grey color and large dewlap; while the Patagonian gives a rough coat and ears that are slung most anyway from the proper position. These crosses all give excessive weight and are employed for that purpose when breeding for market purposes. In mating, whatever is done, we ought to bear in mind that we are not making a variety, but are trying to excel in the quality of a specimen of a present variety.

When we have excellent specimens from the best blood procurable, we should use our own stock for mating, utilizing the best of each litter, gradually building up a strain fit to win in any company. Having a type in our mind, and mating for that type, we can quickly succeed in securing an ideal for the market or for exhibition. Many fanciers erroneously place all their confidence in the buck. The breeder who insists on a good doe with a good buck is the winner. Rather a good doe than buck when only one is available; so go in for a good doe, and when you have her do not breed her to death, nor underfeed her when with a litter of young. The greatest difficulty is in the selection of colors. Other properties being equal in male and female, you must strike a balance—you must take light and the dark. Don't mate two of the same shade unless they have a certain qualification you do not otherwise possess. Try and mate one deficient with one fully developed in that deficiency; that is striking a balance; always taking care not to lose what has been obtained by previous matings.

BREEDING.

For those who breed for profit there are two courses open —one is to keep all the stock until fit for exhibition, or for sale at fancy figures; the other is to market at from four to six months of age. In either case the methods are so similar as to not require any special explanations.

The doe has visited the buck and is placed in the hutch where she is expected to rear her prospected family, which is expected in thirty days from the date of the visit to the buck. She must be supplied with an extra amount of food and green stuff, and a couple of days before the time is up, give an extra quantity of straw or hay to built her nest with; leave no loose dishes or other articles in the hutch, for she may utilize them when building.

It should be observed that during the whole period of pregnancy the doe should be kept as quiet as possible. Be sure and have a supply of water in the hutch at the time of kindling; this is very important and no doubt it prevents many does from destroying their young as soon as born. At this time there seems to be an unusual thirst, and in their frenzy they destroy their young to appease their inordinate thirst. Confirmed killers have been completely cured by the observance of this rule. Young does sometimes kill their first litter or neglect them, but this is not liable to occur again; do not condemn them too soon.

Do not molest the nest for two or three days; when, after carefully removing the doe from the hutch, giving her a run on the rabbitry floor, you may examine the young at your leisure, removing any dead or extra youngsters you do not care to raise—five or six are enough. Do not handle them more than is necessary. Give the doe a carrot or some dainty she will eat, after an hour or two replace her in the hutch, and she will be so anxious to nurse that the intrusion is seldom noticed. Feed her as usual, giving an extra quantity of food and green stuff, for the young grow fast and if the doe is not well cared for, she, in turn, cannot do justice to her young; and they will have slobbers if not sufficiently nourished.

In two or three weeks the young will be moving about the hutch; from now until weaned is the critical time in their existence. With the food and care recommended they will prosper. When about two months old they should be taken from the doe and allowed to run on the rabbitry floor; the doe being started for another family. In cold weather a nest box is good for the young litter; place it in a corner so in their gambols they are not liable to run against it. A large soap box with the top taken off and a hole five inches square in the end answers very well. In the summer such a nest would cause bad ears from the excessive heat. Feed them hay, whole oats, stale bread, cooked potatoes, etc., a limited supply of green food and fresh water every day; bread and milk, not sloppy, is an excellent food for growing youngsters.

Separate the sexes when taken from the doe, and at four months of age separate the males, as they get quarrelsome and the weaker ones are completely ruined sometimes in their fights. Do not breed a doe under seven months of age, and not over four times a year; by this arrangement she will raise strong, healthy litters until four or five years of age. For breeding purposes an old buck and a young doe beget the largest young.

THE NURSE DOE

Is often employed in assisting the more valuable varieties to raise all their progeny. The plan followed is simple and effective. A Dutch doe makes the best nurse. They are struck by an inferior buck at the same time as the more valuable doe, so that when the exchange is made the nurse doe's young are all destroyed, and she is given half of the young from the other doe. Exercise the same care in handling. They are wonderful milkers, often rearing larger young than the larger doe.

Help the nursing doe all you can; she is the prime factor of your success, by giving the youngsters a start. Bread and milk is excellent food for her and the young.

KEEP A RECORD.

The general plan of the record is simple in detail and effectual in its results. The great thing in system, which must be vigorously followed or disagreeable mistakes will occur, generally too late for reparation.

I keep a record book of my rabbitry, in which is recorded every incident concerning its occupants. Aside from the entries from time to time of the ordinary *Dr.* and *Cr.*, items and occurences of unusual importance, I have a record of every animal, its pedigree, matings and its final disposition, and can, at glance, give any information required. The accompanying tabulations are actual copies from my record book in use at the present time.

When a rabbit becomes of an age sufficient for breeding, it is given a number and a name, the number follows consecutively, regardless of sex, and are recorded thus:

No	Sex.	By Doe.	Buck.	Born.	Name.	Remarks.
11	Bk.	Imported.	Imported.	Dec. '92,	Business.	First World's Fair. Oct. 1893.
13	Doe.	2	7	Mar '93.	Cinch.	Sold October 1, 1893.
18	"	Imported.	Imported.	June '93.	Eureka.	....

If a doe, she is placed in a hutch and a card is attached, showing her name and number. The bucks are not recorded unless sold or selected for breeding. When the doe has visited the buck another card is attached to the hutch, which shows the date, number, etc., viz.:

O.
Doe 18.
Buck 20.
Dec. 3, 1893.
Due Jan. 3, 1893.
F.

The large letter F at the bottom of the card is the mating check letter in the Record Book, and by looking at the mating F the comparison is easily made. The record of matings are made thus:

MATINGS.

Letter.	Doe.	Buck.	Date.	Tested.	Due.	Remarks,
E	10	11	Nov. 27	No.	....	Sold December 1.
F	18	20	Dec. 3.	Dec. 15.	Jan. 2.	Had nine young, put five to nurse.
G	19	11	Jan. 25.	Jan. 30.	Feb. 14.	Sold February 5, 1894.

The pedigrees are arranged thus:
    No. 8. Doe, "Helderberg," Sept., 1892.
        Sire, Imported Rufus x dam, Altomant.
        She by Big Pete x Donavan doe.
        Their parents imported in 1890.

PREPARING FOR EXHIBITION

Requires some extra labor, and more exercise for the spec-imens under preparation. The majority of rabbits are shown too fat; they must be worked down; they must be groomed daily; restrict the green food also; get them into that race-horse shape required in the exhibition specimen.

A buck which has become bunchy, no matter how he ex-cels in other points, cannot enter the show with an equal chance with the long slim built animal. The doe which has become baggy from excessive breeding is also handicapped. Immature specimens should not be shown, as they give the stranger an erroneous impression regarding their size, which is hard to eradicate.

DISEASES OF RABBITS,

Although a list, few are encountered by the American fancier, while the foreign fancier contents with many not enumerated here. Our climate and our abundance of every-thing that a rabbit will eat together with our American fash-ion of not allowing ourselves to be tied down to the lines drawn by our grandfathers, all tend to make life much more bearable for our furry pets.

When you see your rabbit sitting and moping in a corner, paying no regards to his meals, etc., you may rest assured that it is not in good health, and you should immediately try and find out the reason and apply the remedy.

Let me impress upon your minds that in all cases "Prevention is better than Cure" and if rabbits are kept in condition in well ventilated hutches, dry and warm, supplied with suitable food, they often go through their lives without having a single ill.

The prescribed treatment is founded on actual experience, and it is hoped that this article will enable the fancier to understand the various ills, and apply suitable remedies.

APPETITE, LOSS OF

Is due to various causes, generally a simple cold or its digestive organs may be disordered.

Treatment:—Keep the rabbit warm and give a little stimulant to drink such as mulled ale, or a little sweet wine, tempt with some delicacy such as a piece of carrot, bread and milk, steamed corn, with a few tea leaves mixed in, if in the summer give a little dandelion daily.

BLINDNESS IN THE YOUNG.

Can often be traced to filthy hutches or some projecting nail or wire. When the hutches are neglected the filth develops noxious gases which tend to inflame their eyes often causing total blindness, they appear swollen and often red pimples are to be seen around the lids.

Treatment:—Isolate the rabbit, taking care that the hutch is warm. Bath the eyes with a lotion of ¼ oz. of sulphate of zinc to a pint of water, apply two or three times a day with a soft sponge.

CANKER

In the ear is a very uncommon disease and one quite difficult to cure, the symptoms are a thick yellow discharge from the inside of the ears and sometimes from eyes also.

Treatment:—Clean out the ear with a small soft sponge fastened to a stick soaked in warm water, wiped dry carefully and wash out with the zinc lotion, twice a day, cleanse the animals bowels with cabbage leaves or small dose of flowers of sulphur in its food.

COLIC.

Is a painful contraction of the bowels due to indigestion or from constipation, the animal is restless and the belly seems to be more or less distended with wind.

Treatment:—Dissolve a Beechams pill in water, say two teaspoonsful, give half at a dose once a day until the bowels act freely, feed carefully for a few days, giving little green stuff.

CONSTIPATION.

Is not generally difficult to cure it is caused by an excess of food.   The rabbit is seen to mope in the corner of the hutch, and refused to eat, yet seems often very thirsty.

Treatment:—Give the pill solution until the bowels act freely, feed bread and milk or green food being careful not to cause the other extreme.

DIARRHOEA,

The passage of loose watery stools more frequently than is natural constitutes diarrhœa, and may result from several causes such as a chill, excessive heat. a fright or a too liberal supply of green food when unaccustomed to it.

Treatment:—Remove the Rabbit to a dry warm hutch, and take an ordinary dose (for a grown person) of any favorite "cholera cure" add to one teaspoonful twelve or fifteen teaspoonsful of water, mix well, give the effected animal a teaspoonful every three hours until an improvement is noticeable. Supply with dry oats, bread or clover hay, allow a little milk or water, but no green food until recovery is assured.

An over supply of succulent food to young growing stock is often the cause of

DROPSY,

The belly becomes swollen and hard and for a time does not seem to seriously effect them, but soon they loose their relish for food and if not relieved will gradually pine away and die.

Treatment:—Remove to a large airy hutch where they may have more exercise or let them run on the rabbitry floor, feed them dry bread, oats, cracked peas, hay (not clover), water once a day and occasionally a carrot or turnip, rigidly excluding the green food until health is regained.

EAR GUM.

The ears should be occasionally examined to see if they are free from dirt and wax, when suffering from this trouble they shrink from being handled, as it no doubt is painful for them.

Treatment:—Syringe the ear carefully with warm water and glycerine, care being taken not to inject too forcibly, dry with a soft sponge and apply some simple ointment daily, avoid handling by the ears at all times as heavy specimens are often seriously injured by so doing, causing serious inflammatory conditions so difficult to eradicate.

FITS.

Or convulsions are most commonly met with in young stock and generally can be traced to some irritating cause, such as indigestion or over feeding.

Treatment:—Keep the affected rabbit warm, and dry and give the following pill: Sulphate of iron 1 grain; extract of gentian 2 grains, to make 1 pill. One to be given twice daily. Give plenty of good nourishing food and exercise.

SORE HOCK.

Is generally caused by filthy hutches, dampness and sticks or slivers in their litter, those who use sawdust or machine shavings for litter can easily trace the cause of their troubles, improper feeding will debilitate and lower the vitality necessary to heal the wounds inflicted by their stamping while the damp filth will prove a continuous irritant.

Treatment:—First clean the hutch thoroughly, then whitewash, provide a good bed of hay or oat straw, wash the affected parts in warm water, dry thoroughly, apply carbolized vaseline, in an aggravated case put on a bandage being sure to sew it on not leaving any ends for the animal to nibble on. Give good wholesome food and water or bread and milk.

INSECTS,

are generally traced to neglect.

Treatment:—Is simply cleanliness and sanitation. Carbolized whitewash is recommended.

MANGE,

Is caused by a parasite which barrows in the skin and is analogous to the itch in man. Sulphur is considered a specific in man, so it must follow the same in the rabbit.

Treatment:—Isolate the rabbit and apply the following ointment: Flowers of Sulphur 1 oz., Lard 4 oz. mix I have been unusually successful in treating mange in dogs, cats and rabbits, with carbolized vaseline, the animal does not lick it off as they will the sulphur mixture and it is certainly much easier applied. In every case thoroughly cleanse the hutch containing the affected animal.

PARALYSIS,

This disease generally attacts the hind quarters and renders them quite useless. The cause is generally traced to uncleanliness and damp floors.

Treatment:—Keep the rabbit warm and furnish nutricious food, also remove all filth in the hutch and disinfect thoroughly, give twice a day a pill as follows: Tartrate of iron 20 grains, Quinine 10 grains, extract of gentian 20 grains; mix, make into 10 pills.

RED WATER,

Or as is often called bloody urine, is an affection of the kidneys and has no general symptoms except as stated and if allowed to go on will cause a rapid decline and end fatally.

Treatment:—Care in food, fresh air and a warm even temperature. Give 10 drops of the following twice a day in water, sulphuric ether ½ oz., tinc. gentian ½ oz., tinc. ginger ½ oz.; mix.

SNUFFLES OR INFLUENZA.

In the English breeders hutches, snuffles is almost always present, and is invariably fatal if not promptly attended to, the American fancier is often troubled with the disease but it seldom is as virulent as our foreign friends find it. Just as a man neglects his own person when suffering from a cold, so is the person apt to neglect the rabbits. But a cold is always a matter of concern in a rabbit, and should receive immediate attention. The symptoms of snuffles are sneezing, moist nostrils, which in a few days become thick and filthy, refusal of food and its coat becomes rough and disordered giving every sign of illness and discomfort.

Treatment:—Wash the nose and mouth well with carbolic soap also the fore legs and feet two or three times a day, wipe dry and put an extra quantity of fine hay in the hutch, keep in a cool airy place and feed stimulating foods. Where this course does not effect a cure, the following favorite English prescription is recommended, which must be used in an ordinary vaporizer: Fill the vaporizer about two-thirds full of boiling water into this pour ½ oz. of soluable sanitas oil, 1 teaspoonful of oil of eucalyptus and 10 drops oil of camphor, place the top on and light the lamp underneath. Place the rabbit in a small hutch, covering up with old sacks to prevent the escape of the steam. Insert the spout of the vaporizer into the lower part of the hutch allowing the steam to enter. By this treatment it is intended to have the medicated vapor reach the affected membranes by inhalation. Treat in this manner for ten or fifteen minutes, care being taken that the invalid is not suffocated by the operation, after treatment leave the rabbit in the hutch for a half an hour, then remove as previously advised. It is said that three operations generally effects a cure. In severe cases three drops of eucalyptus and glycerine in equal parts, give in a spoonful of milk for a few days is recommended.

VENT DISEASE,

occurs in does and is traceable to improper pairing. It is very troublesome to cure, but if taken early and attended to patiently a cure is usually effected in a few days.

Treatment:—Isolate the effected rabbit and apply carbolated vaseline twice a day rubbing it well in to the affected parts. Do not mate until entirely cured as the trouble can be spread indefinately by a brood buck.

In conclusion I wish to bring to notice and in almost every case the trouble can be prevented, as has been stated previously we have reason to be thankful that so few of these diseases are found in this country. But that fact does not secure immunity. We must be cautious in feeding, secure ventilation without draughts, and enforce a rigid regime of cleanliness, if we wish to go through the hot summer months with the health of our pets unimpared, build up your does weakened from excessive breeding by allowing a rest in summer. You will have just as many rabbits next January, by so doing, and I assure you that you will have fewer dead and stronger living ones.

THE BELGIAN HARE RABBIT.

THE BELGIAN HARE RABBIT is said to have originated in Belgium, where they are now found small in size, but grand in color and markings. They are also found in France, Flanders and Germany in various stages of imperfection. They are called Belgian Hares, simply on account of their resemblance to the hare.

It was for a long time supposed that this valuable rabbit was a cross between the hare and the rabbit. This is not so, and all attempts to produce the hybrid have either resulted in a failure or the production of a sterile mule. The habits of the hare differ so materially from those of the rabbit that the crossing is effected with great difficulty.

The hare is born fully developed with eyes open, and can run about and eat almost immediately; while the rabbit comes into the world blind, naked and helpless, and does not venture from the nest until from two to three weeks of age. The hare nests on the ground, in some sheltered location, never burrowing; while the rabbit always burrows in the wild state and will when in captivity, if allowed.

The Belgian of to-day shows the improvement attainable by judicious and systematic breeding; foremost in importance is their increased size and prolificacy. As the modern Belgian is distinctively a production of the English fancier, the English standard of excellence will be our guide in describing its characteristics as a distinct variety.

To properly describe the Belgian Hare is difficult, especially the color. "Rufus-red" is a redish tan, clear and bright, showing the clearest on the top of the neck and fore shoulders of the animal. The ticking consist of each hair of the animal's coat being tipped with black, which, according to its density and distribution, its value is governed. The more mottled or wavy it appears, the more points are secured. Starting at the shoulders, the color shades darker back over the back and sides, showing the ticking in its finest markings; the haunches are of a gray shade, but showing a distinct brownish cast, they being usually well marked with a wavy ticking.

The head and ears have a dark shading, but no distinct ticking, it being so evenly distributed as not to be called ticked. The head is not large in proportion to the body; it is carried well up and graceful. The forehead is flat and very prominent over the eyes, giving them a very prominent appearance. The eyes are bold, round, and of a dark brown color, possessing a wonderfully pleasing and contented expression. The ears, about five inches long, set up firm, close together, and leaning slightly back, having an edging of black over the tips and extending well down the edges. This edging is termed lacing and is a characteristic of this variety.

The fore feet and legs are small and delicate, and are kept well under the animal, are well colored and *free from white*.

The belly and the underside of the tail are white, preferably with a brownish cast.

The hind feet and legs are large, strong and powerful; while generally lighter in color than the fore feet, they must show no white on the outside or top; for the slightest white on the face, legs or body of a Belgian Hare is a disqualification.

Shape in the Belgian is, aside from color, the chief attraction in appearance, and it is difficult to secure and maintain. The Belgian should be long and slim in build, long and fine in bone, narrow in front, long and lean in the head—in fact, a rabbit calculated to give the observer the impression of speed. This length characteristic to be accompanied with a corresponding gracefulness and symmetry of form. The angular, gawkey, stumpy, or mule-like forms being decidedly objectionable.

The English standard for weight is about eight pounds, which could, in this more favorable climate, be made more, say nine pounds, with sacrificing other valuable points. Specimens are occasionally shown weighing from ten to eleven pounds. No objection should be made to this excessive weight; provided, however, their characteristics are maintained. As a rule the heavy specimens are very faulty in color and form, also often possessing a well developed dew-lap. Coarse, heavy head and ears, bad feet and stumpy forms are too often seen in these elephantine specimens. Belgians should not have a dew-lap and the exhibition specimen is cut five points when possessing such an appendage.

Belgians though not so showy as some of the smaller breeds, by reason of their self color, are noble looking animals, and for domestic use are of greater value than any of their companions. They are hardy, and few are born that will not with ordinary care and attention be reared to maturity. They are unusually prolific, producing from six to ten young at a litter, and will breed from six to eight times a year. They are very docile, much more so than the smaller varieties, and do not consume as much food as is expected for their size.

Of all domestic breeds the flesh of the Belgian tastes the most like the hare and has not the rank flavor so common in the ordinary rabbit. They will live and thrive in woods or warrens, when turned down for breeding at six or eight months old, if some protection be given them from the inclemencies of our seasons.

THE ENGLISH STANDARD FOR THE BELGIAN HARE.

1. *Color*—Rich rufus red (not dark, smudgy color), carried well down sides and hindquarters, and as little white under the jaws as possible............ 20
2. *Ticking*—Rather wavy appearance and plentiful.... 15
3. *Shape*—Body, long, thin, well tucked-up flank and well ribbed up; back, slightly arched, loins, well rounded, not choppy; head, rather lengthy; muscular chest; tail, straight, not wry, and altogether of a racy appearance............................ 20

4. *Ears*—About five inches long, thin, well laced on tips and as far down outside edges as possible; good color inside and outside and well set on......   10

5. *Eyes*—Hazel color, large, round, bright and bold...   10

6. *Legs and Feet*—Forefeet and legs, long, straight, slender, well colored and free from white bars; hindfeet, as well colored as possible..............   10

7. *Size*—About eight pounds............   5

8. *Condition*—Not fat, but flesh firm like a racehorse, and good quality of fur..........................   5

9. *Without Dewlap*..   5

Total............... 100

BLACK BELGIANS.

Breeders of Belgian Hares frequently are surprised by the advent of one or two Black young one in a litter and often they hasten to destroy the stock as impure, the following article taken from the leading English authority on Belgians will I think clear away the doubt to many:

"The value of Black Belgian Hares for stud purposes is very imperfectly understood. As you are aware the old breeders make very successful use of them, as black is part of the color of a Belgian, at times they are likely to throw a black. For many reasons they are invaluable, they are useful to mate to does lacking tone and too light in color, they also infuse new vigor in their offspring, they are always the most healthy, the strongest, and the most precocious of the litter. *But why are they black?* In making the belgian a Belgian, black blood was introduced for just the purpose stated, and now that nature having all its force and energy concentrated, he reversion is accounted for.

THE LOP-EARED RABBIT, until recently, was the most
popular of the fancy varieties, the peculiar formation of its
ears being its chief attraction.   They have enormous droop-
ing ears, often measuring twenty-two or more inches from
tip to tip and are often over six inches in width, this ear
development being of the greatest importance in the breeder's mind.   They have not yet become popular in this country, probably on account of requiring so much attention and
care, they have become, by years of breeding, a hot-house
variety.   The hutch must be kept warm and in the cooler
months, artificial heat must be supplied.   The Lop generally
possesses a large dew-lap, which is not an objection, other
points over-balancing.

In self colors they are found black, grey, white, blue,
fawn and yellow.   In broken colors, combinations of white
with any of the above, and even a mixture of black, fawn
and white, are found making the tortoise shell.

Lops often weigh from sixteen to seventeen pounds, and
even eighteen pounds is recorded.

THE DUTCH RABBIT, though much smaller yet none the less popular, is a comparative stranger to this country. They are very pretty and useful; the size is bred down by the exacting fancier, their weight being limited to five or six pounds. Their ears are just the reverse of the Lop, standing erect and being quite short. They are unusually prolific and hardy and will breed eight or ten times a year, raising eight to ten young at a litter. On account of their wonderful milking proclivities they are selected as nurse does where more valuable stock is to be raised. In colors they range over the same as the Lops and have a characteristic marking of white in the shape of a broad band or collar around the body at the shoulders and a white blaze in the face; in the old style this collar being much larger than in the new style, which covers only the neck and forward toes.

THE SIBERIAN RABBIT in perfection should resemble both the Himalayan and the Angora, having the Himalayan markings and the Angora's fleece. Most specimens shown are but crosses of the two varieties.

THE HIMALAYAN bids strong for popularity on account of its beautiful markings. The body is white and the fur short and fine, while the ears, nose, feet and tail are dark nut brown, almost black; the eyes are red, the ears are very short and firm. They Weigh from five to seven pounds and are extremely hardy and quite prolific.

THE EGYPTIAN RABBIT is a new comer; resembling the Himalayan so closely that the assertion that they were of no relation was received with doubt. They weigh from eight to ten pounds and are hardy and prolific. The body is white, with black ears, nose, feet and tail; it has also a black ring around each eye and a black stripe extending along the back. Where first brought to notice in France, they are said to be a superior article of food, fully equalling any of its competitors.

THE JAPANESE RABBIT appeared simultaneously with the Egyptian and is thought to be allied to the Dutch, though claimed to be a distinct variety. Some shown in Paris, in 1888, were of the true tortoise shell color, which is black, fawn and orange—no white, as in Lop or Dutch markings.

The head and ears were beautifully striped, as were the feet. The specimens shown weighed about ten pounds each and were said to compare favorably with the other breeds in hardiness and prolificacy.

THE ANGORA RABBIT is deservedly popular wherever bred; they occupy a distinct place in the fancy as a freak of nature that is at once ornamental and useful. The coat of the Angora is its chief attraction, being composed of long, fine, fleecy wool, making them appear to be of prodigious size, when in reality they are no heavier than larger specimens of the Dutch. The most valuable are the white with pink eyes, although colored ones are frequently selected. They are good breeders and attentive mothers. Especial care must be taken to keep the hutch clean and well supplied with clean hay or straw, and their fleeces kept free from knots and filth.

THE POLISH RABBIT is pure white, thin, pink ears, color-less eyes, and altogether a delicate, timid animal. They are said to have originally been found in Poland; but every

investigation seems to prove that they are but Albinos, in-
bred until all vitality and hardiness has been bred out. They
are indifferent breeders and inattentive mothers, and can
only be placed as pets.

THE ENGLISH RABBIT, while comparatively unknown here,
is very popular with the English fancier. They are pecu-
liarly marked, reminding one of the coach dog—white with
black spots. The most valuable arrangement of spots are
one on, or one each side of the nose, a ring around each eye,
black ears and tail, black patches along the back and sides
gradually increasing in size from the shoulders back over the
body; the more symmetrically they are arranged the greater
their value. This rabbit is essentially a fancy variety,
and compares well with the other varieties for size and prolificacy.

THE SILVER-GRAY RABBIT originally was a near neighbor
to the Himalayan, and has become a favorite in Europe and
England. They have improved wonderfully in appearance
since their introduction. In color they run from a bluish-
brown through the slates to a black under color. The ideal
rabbit being a dark blue under color and well silvered, with
white hairs tipped with black. They are good breeders and
are hardy, growing to a good size, often weighing ten pounds
at maturity. The Creams and Fawns are off-shoots from
the Silver Grays, and are probably bred and sold as such.
They share the popularity their ancestors enjoyed and are
with them the fanciers' choice in England at present.

THE FLEMISH GIANT RABBIT, aside from the Belgian Hare,
is the most popular of the large breeds. It is claimed by
some that the Flemish is an overgrown Belgian, which by
continued selections and breeding has resulted in the present
variety. If this be so, they are far removed: for the Flem-

ish is characteristically a distinct variety. One will meet more Belgian-Flemish crosses than pure blood of either variety. The Flemish stands the only rival to the Belgian and is far behind in popularity at present. The Flemish Giant from twelve to fifteen pounds, and in color is a dark steel-gray; ears about six inches long, carried erect. This variety possesses a large dew lap; eyes dark brown; bull dog shoulders, and massive hind quarters; they are fair breeders and are quite prolific and hardy.

THE PATAGONIAN RABBIT is the giant of the species, averaging from fourteen to fifteen pounds. Some authorities claim them to be an off-shoot of the Belgian or the Flemish. Their color is iron-gray, somewhat tawny, and rough coated; they have large, thick, heavy ears, the tips of which are soft and pendulous, usually they are carried standing out from the head like the letter V. In this variety are found the several styles of lop-ear, namely: half lop, horn-lop, and oar-lop, which are considered very objectionable.

THE RAM RABBIT of Spain resembles the Patagonian, with the exception that the Ram possesses a dew-lap.

THE SWAN RABBIT is similar, except the ears, which are about two inches long. These last two varieties have not been accepted by fanciers yet, therefore our knowledge of them is limited.

THE ST. HUBERT RABBIT is the lord of the fancy in France, where it originated; though only recently perfected, it has become very popular as a fancy and as a market rabbit. The French claim all the good qualities of the other varieties are to be found in the St. Hubert. They weigh from twelve to fifteen pounds and resemble the Belgian Hare in shape.

In color, the body and ears are silver, the nose and belly white. They have two stripes of white across the back, the ears are laced like the Belgian Hare. The matings necessary to produce the St. Hubert are these—

    Silver buck x Belgian doe=A.
    A x Wild Rabbit doe=B.
    B x Flemish Giant doe=St. Hubert.

Five or six years of mating and selecting have fixed the characteristics of this variety as a distinct breed.

Last but not least allow me to introduce the DEAD RABBIT.

This genius is found all over the United States, they are easily recognized whenever encountered, immediately upon a hard working fancier securing a success in his fancy these leeches assume all the responsibility and proclaim to the world that it was their stock, (how modest) which won the victory, they siege upon every occasion to flood the country with the grossest imitations of the genuine article and when brought face to face with their outraged patrons flatly deny any intend to defraud. The Belgian Hare has not escaped these most ravenous of beasts. Care has been taken to exclude all this variety from these pages, hoping the near future will find the Dead Rabbit known only in Ancient History.

                    Respectfully Yours,
Troy, N. Y.   THE AUTHOR.
    June 1st, 1896.

The German Hare.

The German or Belgium Hare is yet but little known in the United States. Wherever tried they have proven to be much more profitable than any other kind of Rabbits, as they are prolific breeders, easily raised and always bring a high price in the markets.

For Price, History and description of the true German or Belgium Hare, address,

SAMUEL WILSON,
MECHANICSVILLE, PA.

Wilson's Seed Catalogue, Plant, Tree and Live Stock Annual Free to all who apply.

REQUA BROS.,
BREEDERS OF IMPORTED

BELGIAN HARES.

We aim to produce that rich fawn, with black ticking at end of each hair. Enclose two cent stamp for information and CIRCULAR.

REQUA BROS.,   **Highland Mills, N. Y.**

ORANGE COUNTY BELGIAN HARE FARM.

Members American Belgian Hare Club

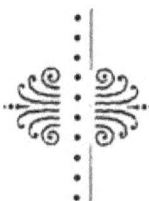

BREEDERS CARDS.

BELGIAN HARES bred in their purity. Fifty pairs for sale. Also Pit Games, by *W. B. Dieffenback*, Angola, N. Y.

W. H. FOUST, Parkesburg, Pa., breeder of Pure Blood Belgian Hares. Also cross-bred Hares for market and table use for sale at moderate prices.

COL. JOSEPH LEFFEL, Springfield, Ohio, is the most extensive breeder of poultry and pets in America. Rabbits, guinea pigs, ferrets, pigeons, dogs, Maltese cats, Shetland ponies. Circulars free.

LOP-EARED RABBITS, pedigreed stock. Flemish Gaints, the finest market rabbit, from imported stock weighing 30 lbs. per pair. Also Belgian Hares, Buff Cochins and Brown Leghorns. *Elliott Smith*, Port Chester, N. Y.

BELGIAN HARES. White Fantail and Homing Pigeons, $1.00 per pair and up, according to age and quality. White Rats and Jap. Rats, each, 20 cts. Guinea Pigs, each, 50 cts. Enclose stamp for reply. *E. F. Barry*, Machias, Me.

COLLINS & WILDER.
48 SPENCER AVENUE. - - - CHELSEA, MASS
—— BREEDERS OF ——

Himalayan and Common Rabbits.
YOUNG STOCK A SPECIALTY.

Write for our prices.

White Plymouth Rocks, .·.

Prizes winners at Jackson, Mich., Jan 7–11, 1896—first on Cockerel; second, third, and tieing first on Pullets; third on Cock; second on Pen, tieing for first.

Eggs for Hatching in season $1 50 for 13; $3.00 for 30. **Stock for sale at all times.** *Address,*

J. J. CLEMENT, South Haven, Mich.

PRINTING

THE AMERICAN STANDARD OF PERFECTION,

AS ADOPTED BY

THE AMERICAN POULTRY ASSOCIATION.

Last edition issued. A complete description of all the recognized Varieties of Fowls. Price by mail postpaid $1.00. Handsomely bound in cloth.

CAPONS AND CAPONIZING.

By GEO. Q. DOW.

A thorough and complete work on these subjects, written by a caponizer who has had years of experience in raising and caponizing cockerels. This book covers the entire field from a to z. Price 25 cents postpaid. Bound in cloth 50 cents.

All About Broilers and Market Poultry Generally.

By MICHAEL K. BOYER.

A thorough, practical and complete work. It contains all you want to know about these very important subjects which so much interest poultrymen generally. Mr. Boyer, the author, is an experienced writer, having written regularly for several years for the poultry departments of some of the leading agriculture and poultry journals. The author has resided in the great broiler town of Hammonton, New Jersey, for several years, and has used every endeavor to get thoroughly posted on the subjects of Broilers and Market Poultry Generally and there is not another place in the world where he could learn so much about these subjects as in Hammonton, where the largest Market Poultry Farms in the world are run successfully. Only 25 cents per copy.

AMERICAN POULTRY ADVOCATE

Published monthly. 20-24 pages, finely illustrated, best writers contribute to its columns, practical articles for all classes of poultry breeders. Gives more reading matter for the money than any other poultry journal published. Also contains a Pigeon and Pet Stock Department. Only 25 cents per year. 64-page illustrated practical poultry book, free to yearly subscribers, mentioning where they saw this offer. Book alone 10 cents. Sworn circulation 12,000 copies or more every month. Four months trial 10 cents. Sample copy free. Best advertising medium, for money invested, known to poultry fanciers. Display advertisements: 10 cents per line; $1.10 per inch, agate type. 14 lines to the inch. Discounts: 3 months 10 per cent., 6 months 15 per cent., one year 25 per cent.

MONEY IN HENS.

By MICHAEL K. BOYER.

This book tells all about the heavy layers, the American class; crossing for eggs; winter layers; houses for winter laying, scratching pens, size of runs, feeding for eggs, pointers from a valuable experience; early hatched pullets; use of two-year-old hens; loss in keeping old hens; market and fancy poultry keeping; keeping down lice—P. H. Jacobs tells all about these pests; preventing sickness; simple remedies for fowl ailments; old and new method of shipping eggs for hatching; an interesting law suit, etc., together with a description of three of the largest poultry farms in this country. Price 25 cents a copy.

Address, CLARENCE C. DePUY, Printer and Publisher,

314-320 E ONONDAGA ST., SYRACUSE. N. Y.

CLARENCE C. DePUY,

Printer, Publisher

And Wholesale Stationer.

320
East Onondaga St.,
Syracuse, N. Y.

✻

WE have a very large collection of Poultry, Pigeon, Pet Stock and Live Stock Illustrations which we can use on any printing you order of us without extra charge. We have unexcelled facilities for getting out first-class printing of all kinds promptly. Five Steam power printing presses. Our prices are very low for first-class work. Letterheads, Cards, Tags, Envelopes, Billheads, etc., printed at prices ranging from 40 cts. per 100 and up, prepaid. Large line of Electrotype cuts for sale. Samples and price list of our work free. Circulars, Catalogues and all kinds of printed stationery executed on short notice.

.˙. PRINTING .˙.

—for—

Poultry and Stock Fanciers

A SPECIALTY.

✻

Publisher of ......

DePuy's Popular Poultry Books and American Poultry Advocate.

See What They Write !

FREEPORT, ILLS., August 25, 1893.

Mr. Clarence C. DePuy,

Dear Sir:—Yours of the 19th inst. at hand, and in reply will say, yes, I will take an one-inch advertisement in your paper for six months, as your paper has brought me many a customer.   Yours truly,

JOHN BAUSCHER, JR.

MOUNT KISCO, N. Y., Sept. 4, 1893.

Mr. Clarence C. DePuy,

Dear Sir:—Please find enclosed 50 cts. for which insert my advertisement three months. Your paper is the best advertising medium I have ever found, one advertisement sold me 15 birds, who can beat that?

Yours, etc.

ELMORE L. REYNOLDS.

SYRACUSE, N. Y., Sept. 1, 1893.

Mr. C. C. DePuy, Pub. AMERICAN POULTRY ADVOCATE.

Dear Sir:—Your favor of the 31st at hand. I am quite surprised at the number of inquiries which I received from my two inch card in your paper and the beauty of it is, most of those who write mean business. This shows that your paper is circulated among a class of people who want to buy, and who have the money to pay. Those are the ones that I wish to get at, and so long as you can bring me in contact with them I shall be glad to remain in your columns. I enclose copy for September advertisement.

Yours very truly,

F. E. DAWLEY.

Harry L. Bell, Mansfield, Ohio, says he sold $5.00 worth of eggs from a 25 cent advertisement in our paper.

J. S. Ferris, DeWitt, N. Y., says he sold $5.00 worth of eggs to *one* customer from a 50 cent advertisement in our paper.

LA GRANGE, IND., Oct. 20, 1893.

Mr. Clarence C. DePuy,

Syracuse, N. Y.

Dear Sir:—The AMERICAN POULTRY ADVOCATE we like very much and think we have been benefited by advertising in it.   Yours respectfully,

MRS. M. L. BELDEN

GOWANDA, N. Y., Oct. 5, 1893.

C. C. DePuy, Syracuse, N. Y.,

Dear Sir:—I received a line from you a few days ago asking the results from my three months advertisement. I can say I was well paid, sold to one man $35.00 worth. Shall be with you again soon.   Very respectfully,

J. D. STUDLEY

DAKOTA POULTRY YARDS.

My breeding birds for season of 1896 are scored by Judge B. N. Pierce, and are mated for best results. Below we give scores of the birds we will use in our yards this season:

CORNISH INDIAN GAMES—Cock, 94; Cockerel, 93½; Hens, 94½, 94½, 93½, 93½, 93, 93, 93; Pullets, 93½, 93. Eggs, $3.00 per 13, or $5.00 per 26.

BARRED PLYMOUTH ROCKS—Cockerel, 93½; Pullets, 93½, 93, 92½, 91½; Hens, 92½, 91½, 90½. Eggs $2 00 per 13, or $3.50 per 26.

WHITE WONDERS—Cockerel, 93½; Pullets, 95½, 93½; Hen, 94½. Eggs, $3.00 per 13; $5.00 per 26.

ROSE COMB BROWN LEGHORNS—Cockerel, 93; Hens, 92½, 92½, 92, 91½, 91½. Eggs, $1.50 per 13; $2.75 per 26; $3.75 per 39.

ROSE COMB WHITE LEGHORNS—Cock, 93½; Hens, 95½, 95, 95, 94, 93½, 93½. Eggs, $1.50 per 13; $2.75 per 26; $3.75 per 39.

BUFF LEGHORNS—Cockerel, 91½; Pullets, 93, 92, 92, 92, 92, 91, 91, 91, 90½, 90½, 90½, 90½, 90; Hen, 91. Eggs, $2.00 per 13, or $3 50 per 26.

I can also furnish eggs from a good pen each of Light Brahmas and Partridge Cochins at $2.00 per 13, $3.50 per 26.

I Guarantee all eggs sent out to be fresh and true to name, and will duplicate a hatch of less than 7 chicks from 13 eggs at *one-half the single setting price*. Eggs at one-half price after July 1st.

WIRE NETTING } Rolls 150 feet long, 4 feet wide, 2 inch mesh, No. 19 wire @ $3.00. Other widths in proportion.

NEPONSET RED ROPE ROOFING } Per roll of 500 square feet, $5.00. Nails and caps sufficient to fasten with each roll.

DEODORIZED BLOOD MEAL { 10 pounds, 50 cents; 50 pounds, $2.00; 100 pounds, $4.00.

LEE'S LICE KILLER { ½ Gallon, 50 cents; 1 Gallon, 75 cents; 5 Gallons, $3.00. Safe to use, easy to apply, and immediate in effect.

REFERENCE, German Bank, Freeport, Ill., or Postmaster, Dakota, Ill.

☞We also breed **BELGIAN HARES** of high quality. Fine young stock for sale at $3.00 per pair.

Inclose 2 cent stamp for our twelve page Circular and Price List. **J. F. SMITH, Box 40, Dakota, Ill.**